Spelling
Skills

KU-491-178

Exercises devised by Nicola Morgan MA
an experienced teacher and educational consultant
Illustrated by Pip Adams

Spelling Skills 7-8 forms part of a home-learning programme designed to help your child succeed at school with the National Curriculum. It has been extensively researched with children and teachers.

This book stands alone as a support for spelling for this age group, but is also a natural follow-on to its companion titles, *Writing Skills* and *Reading Skills*. It covers important aspects of the National Curriculum at Key Stage 2. There is also a corresponding book, *Spelling Skills 8-9*, which completes the programme for Key Stage 2 language.

Good spelling depends on several skills; listening, looking, remembering and practising. All these skills are developed in this book, through structured and enjoyable activities. It is useful to buy or make a small notebook for your child to write the words he or she learns. Use one page of the notebook for each letter of the alphabet.

Encourage your child to use the Spelling Code:
    I. LOOK at a word carefully
    2. SAY the letters
    3. COVER the word
    4. WRITE the word
    5. CHECK the spelling

The level of the spelling exercises is progressive in this book, so try to work through them in order. It is important to stop before your child has had enough and to return at a later date to any exercise that he or she is struggling with.

The fold-out progress chart is a useful record of your child's performance and helps identify his or her strengths and weaknesses. Always reward your child's work with lots of encouragement and a gold star.

When you come to the end of the book, you will find a fun, wipe-clean learning game.

Key to symbols on the page:

 skills covered by each exercise as they relate to the National Curriculum

 notes for parents, explaining specific teaching points

 follow-up activities which will extend your child's understanding of the exercise

commissioning editor: Nina Filipek series editor: Stephanie Sloan
designer: Gail Rose cover design: Paul Dronsfield
Copyright © 1999 World International Limited.
All rights reserved.
Published in Great Britain by
World International Limited, Deanway Technology Centre,
Wilmslow Road, Handforth, Cheshire SK9 3FB.
Printed in Italy
ISBN 0 7498 4007 2

WORLD

Listen, look and learn

To learn different ways of working out how to spell words.

This book has fun exercises to help you spell.

To spell you need to look, listen and remember.

Some words look just as they sound. Spell these.

— — —   — — —   — — —

Sometimes words follow a pattern.
Circle the bit that's the same in each of these words.

bread   head   ready   steady   dead

Now cover them up and spell these.

— — — — —   — — — —

Some words are odd and you just have to learn them, like this:

| LOOK at it | SAY the letters | COVER it | WRITE it | CHECK it |

Try this word.

any   — — —

If words follow patterns, they should be learnt together; help your child practise the LOOK, SAY method. It's important to COVER, not copy the word, as it helps him or her remember it.

To learn to spell words by listening to their sounds.

Listening to sounds

Let's practise spelling by listening to the sounds of these words:

j _ _   s _ _   b _ _

m _ _   r _ _   z _ _

Now listen to the words you've just written.

Can you sort them by sound? Write each word in the correct list.

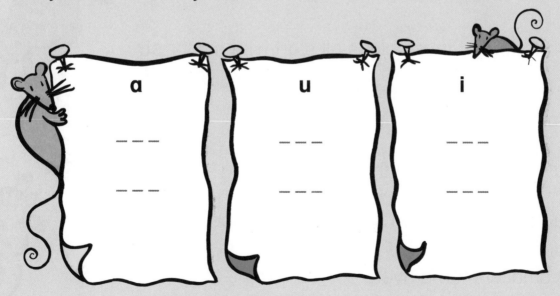

a

_ _ _

_ _ _

u

_ _ _

_ _ _

i

_ _ _

_ _ _

If your child has problems with these, is it because his or her speech is unclear, or because your child is unsure which letter makes which sound?

Listening to sounds

To learn to spell words by listening to their sounds.

Again, listen carefully. Make sure you notice each sound in the word.

p r _ _

_ _ o g

s k _ _

_ _ o t s

_ _ a i _

Here are two sounds: **scr**   **str**

The answers to these clues all start with **scr** or **str**:

A tiny piece of paper is a _ _ _ a p.

You use this for tying things. _ _ _ _ n g

You use this for fixing something to wood. _ _ _ e w

It is smaller than a river. _ _ _ e a m

If you see something scary you might _ _ _ e a m.

To learn to spell words with
th, sh and ch.

Listening for **th**, **sh** and **ch**

Let's practise these sounds: **th sh ch**. Listen to the difference between them.

Use **th**, **sh** or **ch** to spell these words.

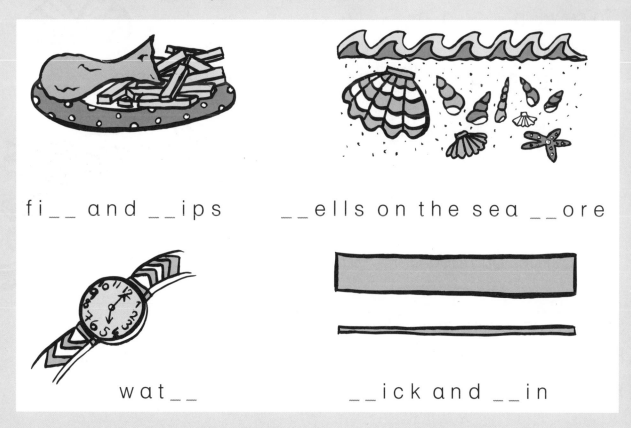

fi _ _ a n d _ _ i p s

_ _ e l l s o n t h e s e a _ _ o r e

w a t _ _

_ _ i c k a n d _ _ i n

The answers to this crossword all have **th**, **sh** or **ch** in them.

1. mice love this food
2. a girl is not 'he' but _ _ _ ?
3. a queen sits on one
4. the opposite of poor
5. use this to wipe up some water
6. a fruit with a stone in the middle
7. to cut with an axe
8. like a butterfly

Listening for **ee**, **oa** and **ow**

To learn to spell words with **ee**, **oa** and **ow**.

Here are some more sounds to listen for.

Write these words with **ee**.

To sew I n _ _ _ a n _ _ _ l e.
Too many s w _ _ _ _ are bad for your t _ _ _ _.
The king and qu _ _ _ spent a w _ _ _ at their castle.

Write these words with **oa**.

I can't speak because I have such a sore t _ _ _ _ _ _.
Does ice sink or f l _ _ _?
The builder dumped a l _ _ d of bricks on the r _ _ _.

Sometimes letters make different sounds.
Read these **ow** words. Divide them into words with **ow** as in **yellow,** and words with **ow** as in **brown**.

now   snow   crow   window   flower   towel

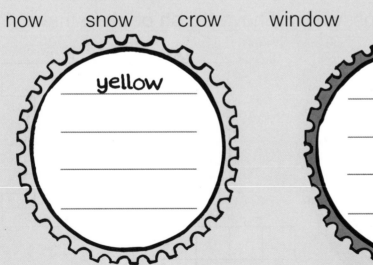

yellow
_____
_____
_____
_____

brown
_____
_____
_____
_____

Learn this odd word: **sugar.**   (Use the LOOK, SAY method.)

6

To learn to spell words with
oi, oy, ai and ay.

Listening for **oi**, **oy**, **ai** and **ay**

Words with **oi** and **oy** sound the same, but we don't use **oi** at the end of a word.

Look at these words.

point   boil   spoil   toy   enjoy   destroy   annoy

Write the correct words in the spaces.

1. You will —————— me if you —————— my —————— .

2. Don't —————— the soup or you will —————— it.

3. I don't —————— it when you —————— at me.

Words with **ai** and **ay** sound the same, but we don't use **ai** at the end of a word.

Finish the spellings and join them to the correct picture:

p _ _ n t

t r _ _ n

b _ _

s n _ _ l

t r _ _

Children need to see how words are made from
roots, by adding beginnings and endings.

Vowels and consonants

To learn the difference between consonants and short and long vowels.

Five letters in the alphabet are called **vowels**: a e i o u
All the other letters are called **consonants**.

Look at these words and circle the vowels.

cat   pocket   eggshell   school

Now circle the letters that are consonants.

s t u g e f r

The vowels can make different sounds. Listen to the sounds that each one makes in these words.

ant	cake
egg	bee
ink	fire
dog	bone
up	cube

When vowels sound like this they are called **short vowels**.

When vowels sound like this they are called **long vowels**.

Knowing about short and long sounds helps children understand many spelling rules.

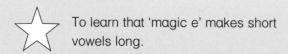

☆ To learn that 'magic e' makes short vowels long.

'**Magic e**' changes the sound of the vowel.
'**Magic e**' makes the vowel sound **long** instead of **short**.

cap + e = _ _ _ _   spin + e = _ _ _ _ _ _

spit + e = _ _ _ _ _   hop + e = _ _ _ _

Can you think of some words with 'magic e'?

_____ + e = _____   _____ + e = _____

All the answers to this crossword have a '**magic e**' making the vowel long.

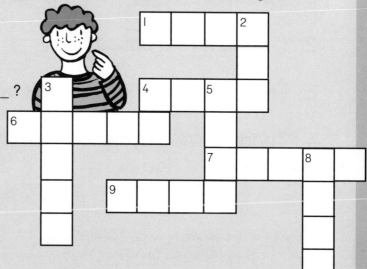

1. a bitter fruit with green skin
2. the day before Christmas is Christmas _ _ _ ?
3. a small rock
4. it belongs to me so it's _ _ _ _
5. in the middle of your face
6. took without permission
7. something very sharp and pointed
8. you need wind to make it fly
9. a piece of glass in a window

9

Learning about syllables

⭐ To learn to break words into syllables.

You can spell long words if you break them into bits.
We call the bits **syllables**.

Clap your hands once for each bit in a word.
Count how many claps.

magnet = mag / net   silly = sill / y   banana = ba / na / na

How many syllables are there in these words?

tickle ☐   sausages ☐   pig ☐   television ☐

Try to spell these words by writing one syllable at a time.

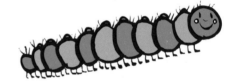

_ _ _ _ _ _ _ _ _ _ _ _ _   _ _ _ _ _ _ _ _ _ _ _

Can you fill in the spaces?

1. I cannot r _ _ _ _ _ e r his name.

2. I would love a baked p _ _ _ t _ for my tea.

3. There's no school next week because we're on h _ _ i _ _ _ .

4. Today we're playing football. Y _ _ _ _ _ d _ y we played tennis.

Sometimes your child will have to choose where to split a word into syllables. Get him or her to choose the place which seems most natural.

To learn to break longer words into syllables.

Let's practise words with more than one syllable.

Can you spell these words by breaking them into syllables? The first one has been done for you.

television	supersonic	recognise

t el/ ev/ i s/ i on _ _ _ _ _ _ _ _ _   _ _ _ _ _ _ _ _

terrible	sausages	telescope

_ _ _ _ _ _ _   _ _ _ _ _ _ _ _   _ _ _ _ _ _ _ _

astronaut	policeman	sister

_ _ _ _ _ _ _   _ _ _ _ _ _ _ _   _ _ _ _ _

Now choose four of those words and learn them, using LOOK, SAY, COVER, WRITE, CHECK .

1 _____

2 _____

3 _____

4 _____

 Using the LOOK, SAY method is very important. If your child keeps getting the same part of a word wrong, ask him or her to over-emphasise those problem letter(s) during the SAY part of the process.

Vowel endings

 To learn to add vowel endings to words.

We can add syllables to the ends of words.
These syllables are called **suffixes**.

Here are some endings. These start with a vowel.

ing   **er**   **ed**

We can make new words by adding them on to other words:

add ► adding   add ► added

jump ► jumping   jump ► jumper

But, if the word ends in **e** and we add an ending which starts
with a vowel, the **e** disappears.

come + ing = coming
hope + ing = hoping
hope + ed = hoped

Fill in the white boxes by adding the endings.
Remember to drop the **e**.

	ing	er	ed
like			
play			
joke			
talk			
double			

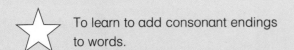 To learn to add consonant endings to words.

Other endings begin with a consonant.

ly   **ful**   **less**   **ness**

For these endings, if the word ends in **e**, the **e** stays.

love + ly = lovely   hope + ful = hopeful

But, if the word ends in **y**, change the **y** to **i.**

happy + ly = happily   beauty + ful = beautiful
penny + less = penniless   happy + ness = happiness

Add **ly** to these words.

love   _ _ _ _ _ _

funny   _ _ _ _ _ _

usual   _ _ _ _ _ _

Add **ful** to these words.

duty   _ _ _ _ _ _

use   _ _ _ _ _

hope   _ _ _ _ _ _

Add **less** to these words.

use   _ _ _ _ _ _

mercy   _ _ _ _ _ _ _

home   _ _ _ _ _ _

Add **ness** to these words

silly   _ _ _ _ _ _ _

black   _ _ _ _ _ _ _

dizzy   _ _ _ _ _ _ _

Practice puzzles

To apply what has been learnt so far.

These puzzles practise words that you have already learnt to spell. If you have forgotten any, you can look back in the book to find the word.

1. We often eat these with fish. _ _ _ _ _

2. You need this to fix something to wood. _ _ _ _ _ _

3. You look through it to see outside. _ _ _ _ _ _

4. The opposite of sink. _ _ _ _ _

How many words can you find with **oi**, **oy**, **ai** and **ay**?

o	p	y	o	l	i	n
b	o	y	i	p	r	o
p	i	a	n	a	p	p
b	n	r	o	y	a	l
o	t	a	i	l	i	a
i	i	o	s	a	n	y
l	o	i	e	i	t	y

Write them all here in your best handwriting.

_____   _____   _____   _____

_____   _____   _____   _____

14

To learn to make words with syllables.

Practising with syllables

These puzzles contain words split into syllables.

Join each jigsaw piece to another to make a word.
Then write the word.

_____

_____

_____

_____

Here are some bits of words. If you are clever you can make
words with three syllables. The first one has been done for you.

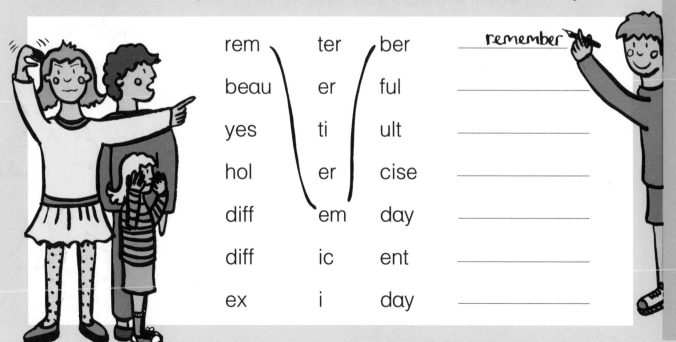

rem	ter	ber	remember
beau	er	ful	_____
yes	ti	ult	_____
hol	er	cise	_____
diff	em	day	_____
diff	ic	ent	_____
ex	i	day	_____

Useful words to learn

To learn some more difficult words.

You have been listening to letter sounds and breaking words into syllables.
But this doesn't work for some very useful words.
You can learn these words using LOOK, SAY…

The words in the balloons are very useful.
When you can spell one, colour its balloon.

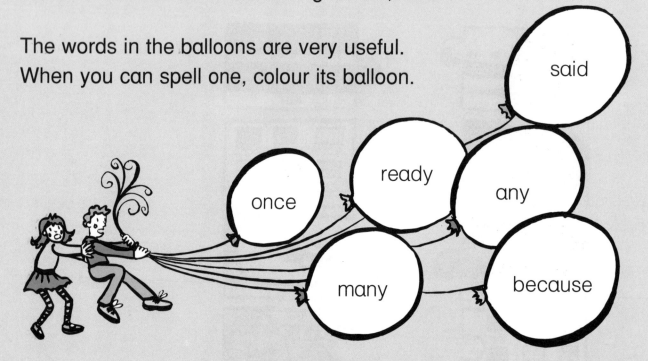

once

ready

said

any

many

because

Make a sentence for each word, like this:

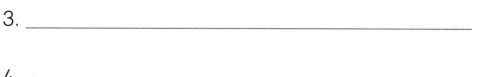

1. My mum **said** you can stay the night.

2. _____

3. _____

4. _____

5. _____

6. _____

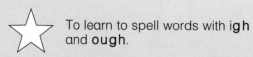

To learn to spell words with **igh** and **ough**.

Do you know this odd pattern: **igh** saying 'eye'?

Read this story, then cover it up and see how many **igh** words you can remember.

Last night I had a fright. Right
outside my window, in the light
of the bright moon, were two cats
fighting: but the oddest thing about
the sight was that both cats wore tights!

_____   _____   _____   _____

_____   _____   _____   _____

These words are odd because they all **LOOK** the same
but **SOUND** different. Ask someone to read them to you:

enough   though   rough

through   cough   tough

I've had e_____ of this awful c_____. It's very t_____

to have a throat that feels so r_____, as th_____ a

cold wind is blowing right th_____ it.

17

Different spelling, same sound

To learn that **ir**, **ur** and **ear** sound the same.

Here are some different patterns which make the same sound. Can you sort the words into the right sacks?

birthday   fir-tree   furry   earth   thirsty   early   circle

heard   surprise   purple   search   dirty   nurse   learn

ir

ur

ear

Here is a funny sentence using the words in the first sack.

On my birthday we danced

in a circle round a fir-tree

until we were dirty and thirsty!

Underline all the **ir** words and draw a picture to go with the story.

To learn some more difficult words.

Choose one of these useful words and write it on the ladder.
Use the LOOK, SAY, method to learn it.
Do the same with the others.

visitor

their

laugh

friend

answer

trouble

pretty

Think of a word which you would love to spell.
Ask a grown-up to write it for you. Learn it in the usual way.

Now you can impress your friends and teacher!

Encourage your child to choose his or her own words to learn. This makes spelling them more fun. It will help if your child writes the new words in a spelling notebook.

Using a dictionary

To learn to use a simple dictionary and arrange words in alphabetical order.

A dictionary is for checking spellings and finding meanings of new words. Words are always arranged in **alphabetical order**.

Put these groups of words in alphabetical order.
If two words have the same first letter, look at the next letter.

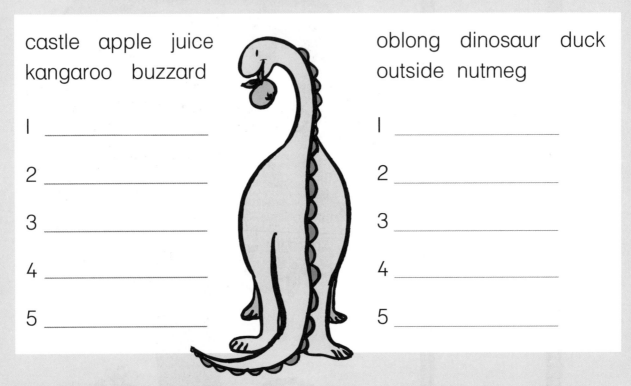

castle   apple   juice
kangaroo   buzzard

1 _____

2 _____

3 _____

4 _____

5 _____

oblong   dinosaur   duck
outside   nutmeg

1 _____

2 _____

3 _____

4 _____

5 _____

Page 32 is a dictionary of the words you have learnt to spell in this book.
Use it to CHECK whether all these words are spelt correctly.

1. kneel
2. ghostly
3. whisper
4. circle
5. volcanoes

6. annoying
7. honest
8. pretty
9. enough
10. thieves

Finding words in alphabetical lists is very important, for using dictionaries and many other sources of information. Always keep practice light-hearted and fun.

To learn to spell words with silent letters.

Silent letters

Lots of words have a letter which makes no sound in that word.

Can you circle the silent letter in each of these words?

reign   kneel   climber   whisper   gnaw   knock   numb

knife   doubt   knowing   honest   sign   hour

Now put each word in the correct rucksack.

Listen... can you hear a **t** in **listen**?

No, you can't, because it's silent.

Write out **listen** three times, saying the letters as you do.

_ _ _ _ _ _   _ _ _ _ _ _   _ _ _ _ _ _

Plurals

 To learn to make simple plurals.

Most words add **s** when you want to turn a **singular** (one) into a **plural** (more than one). But some words do something different.

If the plural sounds as if it has 'is' at the end, add **es**.
fox ► foxes   church ► churches
bus ► buses

If the word ends in a consonant + **y**, drop the **y** and add **ies**.
country ► countries   penny ► pennies

If the word ends in a vowel + **y**, just add **s**.
monkey ► monkeys   tray ► trays

Words that end in **o** USUALLY add **es**.
potato ► potatoes   echo ► echoes

But sometimes we just add **s**.
piano ► pianos   eskimo ► eskimos

Write the plural of these words. If you need to, look at the rule again, but remember to cover it up before you write.

1. donkey _ _ _ _ _ _ _

2. tomato _ _ _ _ _ _ _ _

3. banjo _ _ _ _ _ _

4. pony _ _ _ _ _ _

5. bush _ _ _ _ _ _

6. welly _ _ _ _ _ _ _

7. play _ _ _ _ _

8. toy _ _ _ _

To learn to make more complicated plurals.

There are some other ways in which words are made into plurals.

Words that end in **f** or **fe** usually change to **ves**.

leaf ► leaves   scarf ► scarves   knife ► knives

Some words don't change at all when they are made into plurals.

sheep   deer   aircraft

But some words become completely different.

mouse
woman
foot
tooth

Let's practise plurals!

hoof ► _ _ _ _ _ _

thief ► _ _ _ _ _ _ _

goose ► _ _ _ _ _

tooth ► _ _ _ _ _

volcano ► _ _ _ _ _ _ _ _

mouse ► _ _ _ _ _

Words which sound alike

To learn some words that sound alike.

Sometimes two words sound the same but have different spellings.

witch

which?

Which witch is coming to tea?

Let's learn some more:

here	Look over here!
hear	Didn't you hear what I said?
write	You write very neatly.
right	right and wrong, and right and left
their	I think that's their house.
there	There is a fly on my pizza.

Put the right word in each space.

"Come _ _ _ _, little boy," said the w _ _ _ _,

"and tell me _ _ _ _ _ is the r _ _ _ _ way."

"But where do you want to go?" asked the boy.

Homophones are words which have different
meanings and spellings, but which sound
the same.

To learn some more words that sound alike.

More words that sound alike

blue	The sky isn't blue today.
blew	The wind blew so hard that our roof was damaged.

peace	Peace is the opposite of war.
	Adults like peace and quiet.
piece	Would you like a piece of cake?

four	There are four corners in a square.
for	Come for a walk. It's good for you.

to	I'd love to come to tea.
two	I have two sisters.
too	That's too cold! That one's too cold, too!

Choose the right word from above to fill the space

F _ _ his birthday, Sam took t _ _ friends t _ a restaurant

f _ _ tea. There was an amazing cake with b _ _ _ icing, big

enough f _ _ everyone to have a huge _ _ _ _ _. When he

_ _ _ _ the candles out, he had _ _ have two tries. After tea,

all his friends stayed the night at Sam's house, so his mum

and dad had no _ _ _ _ _!

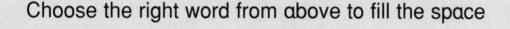

Practice puzzles

 To apply what has been learnt so far.

Let's practise what you have learnt.

How many words can you make using these word wheels?

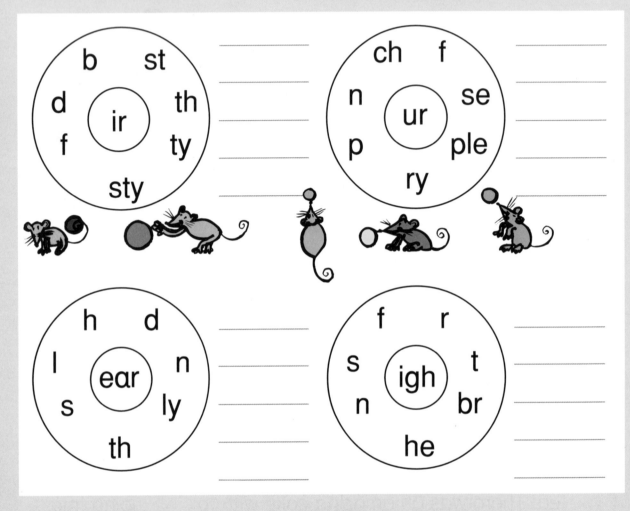

Answer these clues and write the words going downwards.

Which word appears across?

1. difficult
2. not too much or too little
3. you do this if something tickles your throat
4. not smooth

To apply what has been learnt so far.

The words you need to solve this crossword are all on page 21.

Across

1. to go down on your knees
2. this tells you where to go
5. understanding
6. something you cut with
7. not to be sure
8. the time when a king or queen rules

Down

1. to rap on a door
3. someone who goes up mountains
4. if you are this, you tell the truth

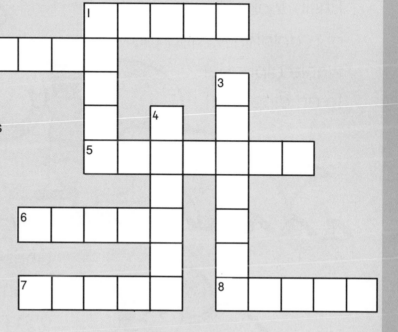

Can you find these words in the word square?

answer   none
any   once
because   pretty
earth   said
friend   their
many   visitor

b	c	e	a	u	v	s	e	o
e	x	e	o	r	i	m	o	m
a	n	o	n	e	s	a	i	d
r	o	a	c	r	i	n	p	h
t	p	r	e	t	t	y	o	l
h	a	r	e	h	o	x	a	i
a	n	s	w	e	r	p	u	s
i	y	f	r	i	e	n	d	h
m	e	o	a	r	b	c	a	s
b	e	c	a	u	s	e	i	d

ph sounds like f

 To learn that **ph** sounds like f.

When **p** and **h** go together they make the sound **f**.

Philip took a photo of a dolphin saying the whole alphabet to an elephant!

Christopher won a trophy when he took a photo of a pheasant on the phone!

Can you spell all the **ph** words you can see on this page?

_____ _____ _____

_____ _____ _____

_____ _____

Phew!

28

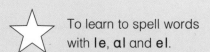 To learn to spell words with **le**, **al** and **el**.

Same sound, different ending

Lots of words end in the same sound as **apple**.

Most are spelt with **le**. But some have **al** and others have **el**.

Sort these words into the correct list.

tickle   cancel   level   unusual   final   travel   apple

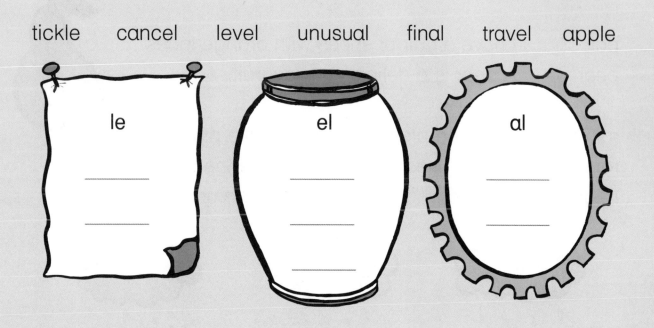

le

_____

_____

el

_____

_____

_____

al

_____

_____

Here's a silly sentence using **le** words.

Little Emily settled down to make a bottle of pickled apples.

Now make up a sentence with the **el** words.

_____

_____

_____

29

More words that sound alike

To learn more words that sound alike.

Here are some more words that sound the same.

whole	I couldn't eat a whole cake at once.
hole	There's an enormous hole in my sock.
pair	I have a pair of shoes with orange laces.
pear	A pear is a delicious, juicy fruit.
rain	We need plenty of rain to make plants grow.
rein	A rider uses the reins to make the horse stop.
reign	Kings and queens usually reign until they die.

Fill each space with the right word.

Each day of the queen's _ _ _ _ _ she

went riding. Even when heavy _ _ _ _

made the _ _ _ _ s wet, she still went

out. Every six months a _ _ _ _

appeared in her leather boots and she

had to buy a new _ _ _ _.

30

To learn to check spellings in a simple dictionary.

Now you can be the teacher!

31

Sally did a spelling test but she found some words difficult. Which words did she get right? You can use page 32 to check, if you like.

tomatoes	☐		reddy	☐
lissen	☐		honest	☐
happyness	☐		flower	☐
annoying	☐		comeing	☐
beautiful	☐		diferent	☐
remember	☐		meny	☐
becaues	☐		enough	☐
circel	☐		house	☐

Write correctly the words she got wrong.

_____ _____ _____ _____

_____ _____ _____ _____

Tell Sally how she can learn words easily and spell them right next time!

Being able to spot errors is very important.

Ask your child to play 'teachers' and find some 'mistakes' that you have made.

31

Dictionary

This is your dictionary.

It contains lots of words you've learnt in this book.

What a lot of words! Did you use it for some of the puzzles?

How quickly can you find these words in the book.

annoying	flower	none	trouble
answer	friend	numb	visitor
any	geese	once	volcanoes
beautiful	ghostly	pianos	wellies
because	gnaw		
bushes	happiness		
circle	honest		
climber	hooves		
come	hour		
coming	house		whisper
deer	kneel	plays	
destroy	knife	ponies	
different		pretty	
difficult		purple	
donkeys		ready	
	knives	remember	
	knock	royal	
	knowing	said	
	laugh	sign	
	listen	teeth	
doubt	magnet	thieves	
echoes	many	tomatoes	
enough	mice	toys	

You can add some useful words which you would like to remember!